Genre > **Expository Text**

Essential Question
How did democracy develop?

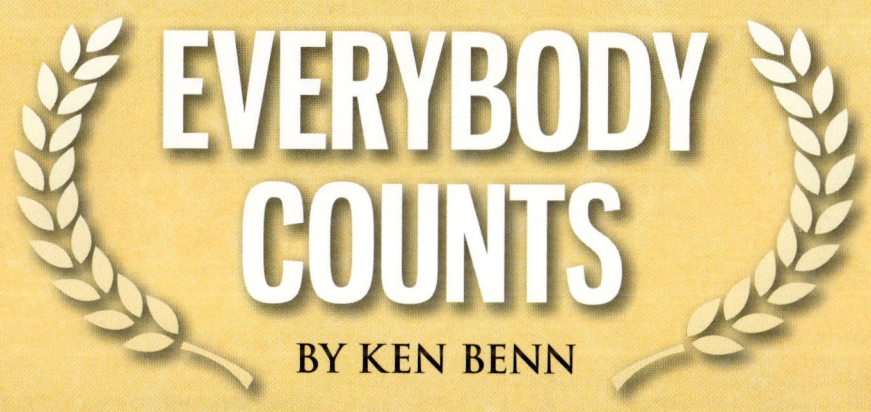

EVERYBODY COUNTS
BY KEN BENN

Introduction	2
Chapter 1 Early Experiments in the Ancient World	4
Chapter 2 Democracy in Europe and Britain	8
Chapter 3 Democracy in the New World	12
Conclusion	16
Respond to Reading	18
PAIRED READ The Men on the Hill	19
Glossary	22
Index	23
Focus on Social Studies	24

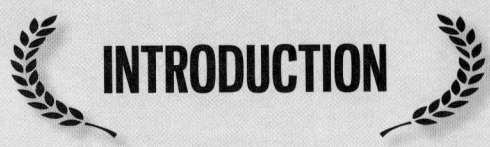

INTRODUCTION

Imagine you are an aspiring voter. You find out that not everyone can vote. You can vote only if your father has the right to vote. However, if your family has lots of money, then you can vote.

This type of voting system doesn't sound fair, but this is how **democracy** began in the ancient world.

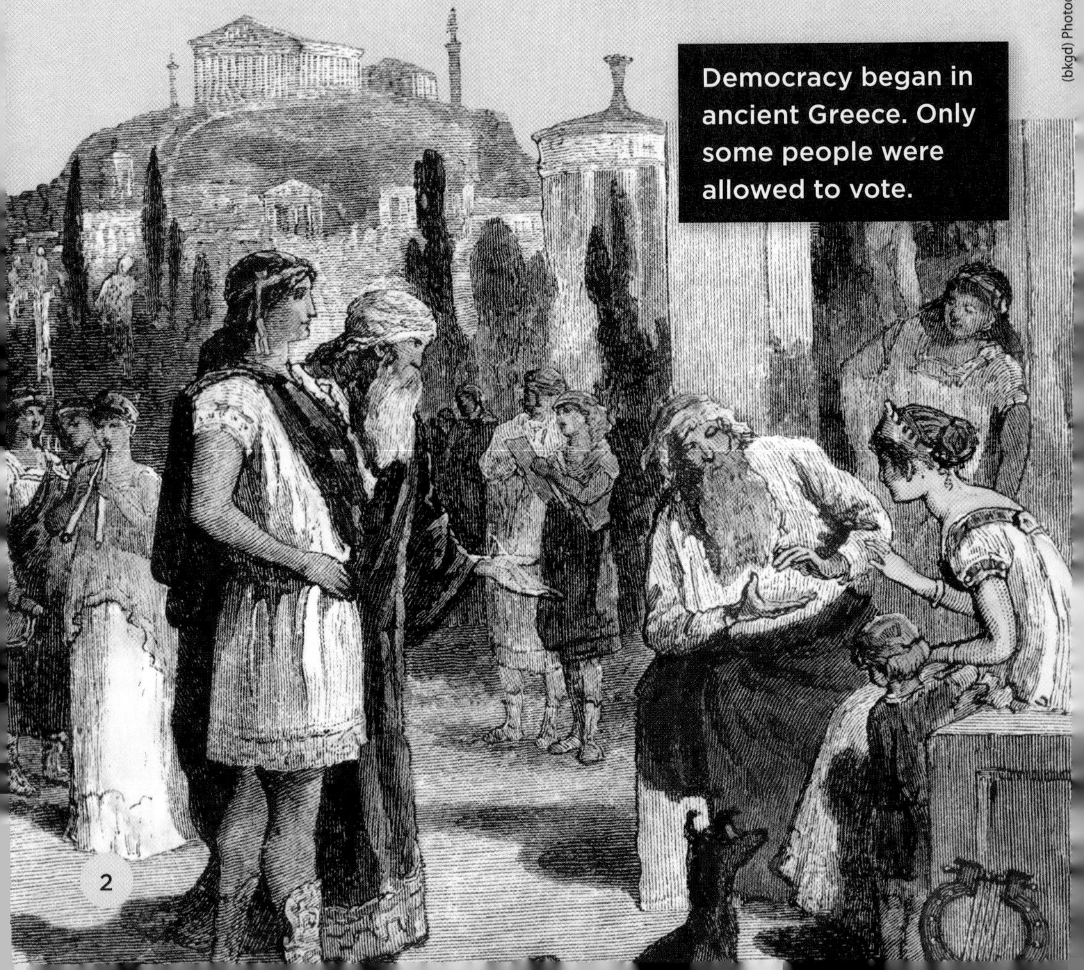

Democracy began in ancient Greece. Only some people were allowed to vote.

(bkgd) Photodisc/Getty Images, (t) Nova Development/Avanquest North America, (b) North Wind/North Wind Picture Archives

The federal government of the United States is based at Capitol Hill, Washington, D.C.

Washington Monument

Capitol building

Lincoln Memorial

    Democracy began in ancient Greece and then spread to Rome. Democracy is a form of government in which people vote for their leaders.

    After the fall of Greece and the Roman Empire, countries in Europe had an **autocratic** system, meaning that one person held all the power. However, the people slowly won certain political rights.

    When the United States of America declared independence from Britain in 1776, it began to rebuild the democratic dream that had begun 2,500 years earlier in Greece. Now we have a country where every man and woman, regardless of their race, class, or religion, has the right to vote.

Chapter 1
Early Experiments in the Ancient World

Ancient Athens is the place where democracy began. Athens was a **city-state** with its own government.

Around 590 B.C.E., only men who owned land had the right to vote for new leaders. Women and enslaved people did not have the right to vote.

By 500 B.C.E., all male citizens had the right to vote. Some of the wealthy people did not like the change. They wanted to choose their rulers and make decisions themselves. They did not want the lower classes to have the right to vote. Leaders who wanted to promote democracy were replaced by autocratic leaders. The people of Athens had to fight wars to remove these leaders.

Rights for Greek Sailors

Greek soldiers had to pay for their equipment, so only the rich could be soldiers. Then Pericles formed the Athenian navy. Pericles was a leader in Athens around 470–430 B.C.E.

The navy needed men to work on the ships. Ordinary men could join the navy. In exchange for their work, the men were given the right to vote.

By 460 B.C.E., it was the ordinary men of Athens who voted on all the important decisions.

The voters were called *ecclesia*. Up to 6,000 voters met on the slopes of the Pnyx hill. The voters elected citizen initiators to start discussions about important issues, such as whether to start or end a war.

Sparta was another city-state located near Athens. The people of Sparta did not support democracy. The Spartans began to feel unsafe about the spread of democratic ideas in the surrounding regions. Eventually Athens and Sparta fought each other in the Peloponnesian Wars. The wars threatened to end democracy. However, democracy lived on in Athens until the Macedonians conquered Athens in 338 B.C.E.

> **In Other Words** continued. En español, *lived on* quiere decir *continuó*.

The Pnyx hill was located southwest of the Acropolis, where the Parthenon is located.

Like Athens, Rome also had a type of democracy. Early in the fifth century B.C.E., the citizens of Rome could vote for leaders of their tribes, called *tribunes*. By 275 B.C.E., the tribunes had become very powerful. The common citizen, known as *plebeians*, could only vote within a tribe. They were restricted from having any real power. Like ancient Greece, women and enslaved people could not vote at all.

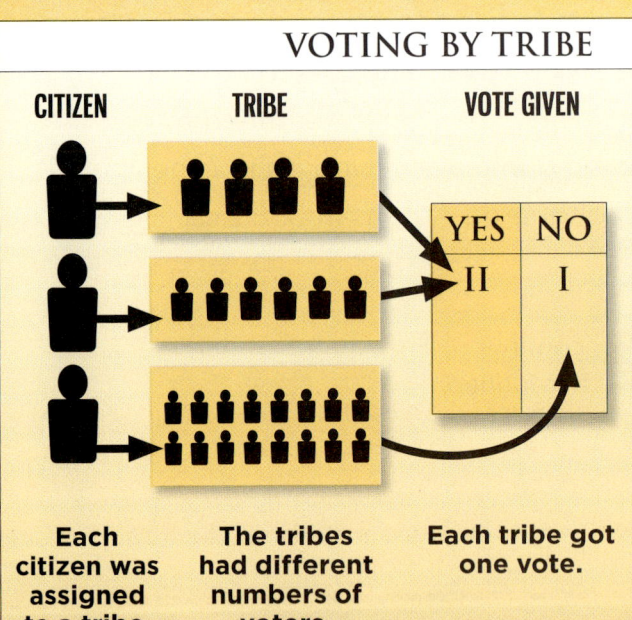

VOTING BY TRIBE

CITIZEN — TRIBE — VOTE GIVEN

YES II — NO I

Each citizen was assigned to a tribe.

The tribes had different numbers of voters.

Each tribe got one vote.

Citizens were only able to influence the voting within their own tribe, so it was possible that two tribes with smaller numbers of members were able to outvote a much larger tribe.

Ruins of the Roman Forum can still be seen in Rome today. Senators, leaders of the *patricians*, the noble and wealthy families of Rome, met there to discuss issues, and the public attended. It was also a market.

In 82 B.C.E., there was a political battle in Rome. The upper classes fought to keep their privileges, while the ordinary people demanded more power. Lucius Cornelius Sulla, a Roman general, became involved in the political battle.

Sulla became **dictator** of Rome, and he killed anybody who tried to oppose him. Sulla changed the political and legal systems. He reduced the powers of the tribunes and gave greater powers to the military.

Rome's experiment with democracy was ending. After Sulla retired, Rome was ruled by a series of dictators, called emperors. This period of dictatorship was called the Roman Empire.

> **STOP AND CHECK**
> Who had the right to vote in the ancient world? Who did not?

ruins

People described Sulla as having the courage of a lion.

CHAPTER 2
DEMOCRACY IN EUROPE AND BRITAIN

The Roman Empire ended in 476 C.E. Autocratic kings became the leaders in the countries that were once ruled by Romans. The kings did not believe in democratic ideas.

By the eighth century, small communities in Scandinavia were exploring the idea of democracy. Male citizens from the communities gathered in groups to make decisions. The groups were called *things*. If the men had to make decisions for more than one community, then *things* gathered to form an *all-thing*.

Communities gathered around a *thing-stone* to make important decisions.

During the Middle Ages (800–1200 c.e.), the city of Venice in Italy became the center for trade between the eastern Mediterranean and northern Europe. Venice began to prosper.

The people of Venice wanted to govern themselves. Like many other Italian cities, Venice formed a people's local government called a **commune**. However, similar to the ancient Romans, the wealthy citizens in Venice wanted to limit the common people's voting rights. They did this by giving the mayor, or *doge*, enormous power. The wealthy citizens chose the doge from among themselves. People were supposed to vote for the doge, but the doge passed his title on to a family member. This practice of choosing family members is known as **nepotism**.

horned hat

cape

This painting by the artist Bellini shows the cape and horned hat worn by all doges.

In the twelfth century, the English kings began to use parliaments. Parliaments were meetings for discussing important political <u>issues</u>. A king would hold a parliament as he traveled from place to place. He would invite important people such as dukes and bishops, and principal representatives of cities and towns, to his parliament.

The cities and town provided military support and money to the king to rule the kingdom. In exchange, the king invited the representatives of cities and towns to his parliament.

> **Language Detective** | <u>Issues</u> is a plural noun. What is the singular noun of issues?

Even though King John put his royal seal on the Magna Carta, he did not intend at first to obey it.

The Magna Carta

In the thirteenth century, England's nobles wanted to limit the king's power. In 1215, the nobles made King John sign a document called the Magna Carta.

The Magna Carta listed the rights of the Church and people. The document said the king had to obey England's laws. It was the first document that restricted the power of a country's rulers. The Magna Carta was the beginning of constitutional, or legal, government.

In the mid-thirteenth century, in France, King Louis IX allowed nobles to hold meetings in his palace. He created the first permanent parliament in Europe. This created speculation that France would have a true democracy. Sadly, true democracy did not occur.

Like Louis IX, King Edward I of England also held parliament. In contrast to the king of France, King Edward I invited both nobles and representatives of the common people to his parliaments. This is how the two British Houses of Parliament, the House of Commons and the House of Lords, began.

Although some countries were moving toward democratic rule, the ideal democracy still had not been created.

STOP AND CHECK

What were the early parliaments like?

The British Houses of Parliament, also called Westminster Palace, are where the House of Lords and the House of Commons meet.

CHAPTER 3
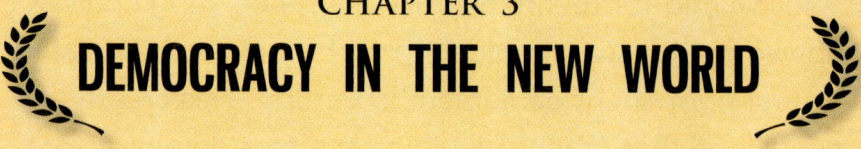
DEMOCRACY IN THE NEW WORLD

"We the people …" are the words that begin the Constitution of the United States of America. These words clearly state that people have the power.

Before the American Revolution, the colonists in America were ruled by the British, but they did not have representation in the British Parliament. After the revolution, the Constitution became the foundation of democracy in the United States.

George Washington became the first President of the United States of America in 1789. This was a great test for the new democratic system. Would the new president become a dictator, or would the people maintain the democratic system?

George Washington was the first president of the United States of America, and he held this office for nearly eight years.

Soon two political parties formed. They were called the Federalists and the Democratic-Republicans. The two parties had very different views about the role of government. The Federalists wanted the federal government to have more power over the states. The Democratic-Republicans wanted the states to have more power than the federal government.

John Adams became the second President of the United States in 1796. Adams was a Federalist. His vice president was Thomas Jefferson, a Democratic-Republican. Jefferson disagreed with President Adams on many occasions, but both leaders followed the ideas of the Constitution. And the new democracy withstood the test.

In 1800, Jefferson and Aaron Burr tied in the election for president. The House of Representatives ruled that Jefferson should be the next president of the United States. This was unlike ancient Rome where a tie would have led to civil war. The new democracy was working well.

Thomas Jefferson was the third president of the United States. He was also a key author of the Declaration of Independence. This document declared that the United States was no longer a part of Britain.

In Other Words
persevered. En español, *withstood the test* quiere decir *perseveró*.

13

Lincoln's handwritten Emancipation Proclamation declared that all enslaved people were now "forever free."

Democracy in the United States was developing, but it did not have **universal suffrage**. Just as in ancient societies, women and enslaved people were not allowed to vote.

Abraham Lincoln was elected President of the United States in 1861. He wanted to end slavery in the United States. Eleven southern states did not want to end slavery. They decided to secede, or separate, from the United States and formed the Confederate States of America. This led to the Civil War, in which the country fought over the issue of slavery. After the war, the Thirteenth Amendment to the Constitution put an end to slavery.

By 1870, amendments to the Constitution were added that made every person born in the United States a citizen.

Language Detective	Societies is a plural noun. What is the singular noun of societies?

Although all women were now citizens, they still did not have the right to vote.

Elizabeth Cady Stanton and Lucretia Mott were two **feminist** leaders who fought for women's right to vote. They held many public meetings and wrote letters to Congress about the unfair political treatment of women.

In 1869, the state of Wyoming preceded the rest of the world by giving women the right to vote. The United States gave the right to vote to all American women in 1920.

> **STOP AND CHECK**
>
> What events helped democracy develop in the United States?

Elizabeth Cady Stanton was the main writer of the Declaration of Sentiments. It states that men and women are created equal.

CONCLUSION

Since its early beginnings in ancient Greece 2,500 years ago, people and societies have wanted democracy. People have had to fight to have a voice in government.

Throughout history people have fought for the rights and freedoms that democracy provides. The American Revolution is an example of people fighting for democracy. It is estimated that more than 60 million people died in World War II, a war that threatened democracy.

Many American servicemen and servicewomen died fighting for democratic freedom during World War II.

The democracy created by the United States of America provides equal rights for all its citizens.

Democracy gives people the right to make their own choices in their lives, including the careers they follow, the religion they practice, and who their leaders should be. Democracy provides freedoms for all.

DEMOCRACY, THEN AND NOW			
CHARACTERISTIC	**ANCIENT GREECE**	**ANCIENT ROME**	**PRESENT UNITED STATES**
Who can vote	Wealthy adult male citizens, then all free adult male citizens	Adult male citizens	All adult citizens
How people vote	Directly	Through representatives (tribunes)	Directly and through representatives
How many votes per person	Based on a man's power and wealth	Based on a man's power and wealth	One
How votes are placed	In person, with a show of hands	In person, with a show of hands	Privately but in person at a polling station, or by mailing an absentee vote

Summarize

Use important details from *Everybody Counts* to summarize what you learned about how democracy developed. Your graphic organizer may help you.

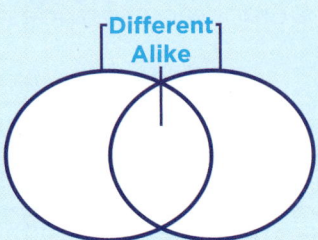

Text Evidence

1. How do you know that *Everybody Counts* is an expository text? Identify the text features that tell you this. **GENRE**

2. What is a key difference between a democracy and a dictatorship? **COMPARE AND CONTRAST**

3. The prefix *in-* means "not." What is the meaning of the word *independence* on page 3? Use the meaning of the prefix to help you figure it out. **GREEK AND LATIN PREFIXES**

4. Compare rule by the people with rule by a king. Write about what might be good or bad about each form of rule. **WRITE ABOUT READING**

Genre > **Narrative Nonfiction**

Compare Texts
Read about voting in ancient Greece.

THE MEN ON THE HILL

> How did the Athenians practice democracy? Follow this story about a farming family who were part of the city-state of Athens.

Dorotheos tried to sleep, but his father yelled, "The cart's loaded and ready to go!"

It was still dark in the hills of Attica. The family was traveling on a rocky road.

Dorotheos's father pointed to a man in the fields. The man was hitching up his plow. "Look at that idiot! He is letting other people make the decisions."

After traveling for three days, Dorotheos and his family reached Athens. His mother said, "I'm not going to the Pnyx hill. I can't vote."

WHO DOESN'T VOTE?

Everybody has the right to vote in a democracy, but some people choose not to vote. Today we say that those people abstain, but the Athenians called them *idiotes*. Dorotheos's father calls the man working in the field an idiot because the man is not going to vote.

Dorotheos asked, "Will I be allowed to vote, Father?"

His father chuckled. "No, son, you have to be 18 to vote."

Dorotheos followed his father to the Pnyx hill. They were ushered to their area on the bare stone.

The farmers were angry as Damon stood on the stone platform. He was the spokesman for the farmers, but Damon disagreed with the farmers about the new tax for olives. So the farmers had come to vote against Damon and the new olive tax.

Dorotheos's father asked other farmers around him, "Do we have enough votes?"

Someone replied, "I don't know. Ioannis couldn't come today."

Damon shouted, "People of Athens! I speak for the farmers."

Dorotheos's father shouted back, "No, you don't!"

Damon explained that the farmers were happy to have the olive taxes raised. He said, "The farmers want to pay their share for the new building projects."

After the speeches, the men voted on the new tax. Dorotheos saw the color of Damon's face turn red as the hands were counted. There were more votes against the tax than for it.

The farmers were able to vote on the new tax. However, it wasn't easy for farmers to get to the Pnyx hill and vote. The farmers had to spend many days traveling instead of working on the farms. The disabled Athenians couldn't climb up to the hill.

In democratic societies today, it is easy for people to vote, no matter how far away they are. All voters are free to use their democratic rights and freedoms.

Make Connections

What does *The Men on the Hill* teach about democracy in ancient Greece? How is it similar to democracy today? **ESSENTIAL QUESTION**

How do the explanations in *Everybody Counts* and *The Men on the Hill* help you to understand how leaders came to power in ancient Greece?
TEXT TO TEXT

Glossary

autocratic a form of rule where one person holds all the power *(page 3)*

city-state a separate state made up of a city and its surrounding land *(page 4)*

commune a group of people who come together to make decisions for a community *(page 9)*

democracy a government decided by a majority of the people *(page 2)*

dictator a ruler with complete power over a country *(page 7)*

feminist a person who believes in equal rights for women *(page 15)*

nepotism using your position or influence to get a job for another member of your family *(page 9)*

universal suffrage the right of all people to vote *(page 14)*

Index

Adams, John, *13*

American Constitution, *12–14*

American Revolution, *12*

ancient Athens, *4–6, 19–21*

ancient Greece, *2–4, 16, 17*

ancient Rome, *3, 6–9, 13, 17*

Declaration
- of Independence, *13*
- of Sentiments, *15*

doges, *9*

Jefferson, Thomas, *13*

Lincoln, Abraham, *14*

Mott, Lucretia, *15*

parliament
- British, *11*
- the first parliaments, *8, 10, 11*

Pericles, *4*

plebeians, *6*

Pnyx hill, *5, 19–21*

Scandinavian politics, *8*

Stanton, Elizabeth Cady, *15*

Sulla, Lucius Cornelius, *7*

tribunes, *6, 7*

Washington, George, *12*

women get the vote, *15*

Focus on Social Studies

Purpose To compare the impact of different forms of government on an individual's life

What to Do

Step 1 Work in pairs to conduct research on ancient Rome or another ancient civilization and learn how people there lived. Then create a character from this civilization. What would this person think about his or her rights? What qualities would he or she want in a leader?

Step 2 With your group, create a modern character, an American who is about to vote for the first time. What would this person think about his or her rights? What qualities would he or she want in a leader?

Step 3 Think of questions that one character might ask the other.

Step 4 Draw the characters. Write down the key points you've discussed with your group next to each character. How are the two characters the same, and how are they different?